pão de queijo
(cheese rolls)

3 cups (450g) sweet manioc starch
½ cup (150g) sour manioc starch
½ tbsp (12g) salt
½ cup (120ml) cooking oil
1 ½ cup (360ml) milk
3 eggs
4 cups (320g) grated hard cheese

In a mixing bowl, mix sweet and sour manioc starch and salt.

In a pan, heat up milk with oil. When it starts to boil, pour the liquid over the manioc starch mix and slowly mix with a spoon. Add eggs and knead for approximately 10 minutes, until smooth. Add cheese and mix thoroughly with your hand, make little balls of dough and distribute them over a baking pan previously greased with oil. Leave some distance between them so they won't stick together when they expand. Bake in a medium preheated oven for approximately 25 minutes, or until the cheese rolls start to become golden brown.

Servings: 80 small rolls
Total time: 1 hour
Difficulty: Easy

madeleines

1 cup (160g) white sugar
1 tbsp (26g) honey
6 egg yolks
1 egg
1 cup (230g) butter
1 cup (135g) potato starch
1 cup (120g) all-purpose flour
6 egg whites
½ tbsp (2g) grated orange zest

With a mixer, beat sugar with egg yolks, honey and egg. Add butter and mix. Add potato starch and flour. When the batter is smooth fold in the egg whites in firm peaks and orange zest.

Pour the batter into an appropriate madeleine pan and bake in a medium-low preheated oven for approximately 20 minutes, or until golden brown.

Servings: 10
Total time: 1 hour
Difficulty: Easy

raisin cake

1 ½ cup (190g) brown sugar
1 cup (230g) butter
5 eggs
½ cup (120ml) sugarcane molasses
½ cup (120ml) milk
2 ½ cup (300g) all-purpose flour
1 tbsp (12g) baking powder
1 tsp (2g) ground cinnamon
½ tsp (1g) ground nutmeg
1 cup (140g) black raisins
1 cup (140g) yellow raisins
1 cup (130g) mixed candied fruits

With a mixer, mix the butter and sugar. Add egg yolks one by one and mix well. Add in molasses, milk, flour, baking powder, cinnamon, nutmeg and mix a bit more. Finally, fold the egg whites beaten into firm peaks. Carefully add raisins and candied fruits (flour the fruits before mixing into the batter). Pour in a greased and floured cake pan and bake in a medium-low preheated oven for approximately 1 hour.

Servings: 12
Total time: 1 hour
Difficulty: Easy

rice flour muffins with coconut

1 cup (160g) white sugar
1 cup (230g) butter
5 eggs
1 cup (80g) dehydrated shredded coconut
½ tsp (2g) salt
1 cup (150g) rice flour
1 tsp (5g) baking powder
shredded coconut for sprinkling

With a mixer, mix the butter and sugar. Add egg yolks one by one and mix well. Add shredded coconut, salt, rice flour and baking powder. Mix until smooth. Finally, fold the egg whites beaten into firm peaks. Fill 2/3 of greased and floured muffin cups with the batter and sprinkle with shredded coconut. Bake in a medium preheated oven for approximately 40 minutes.

Servings: 8
Total time: 1 hour
Difficulty: Easy

guava roll cake

6 eggs
6 tbsp (72g) white sugar
6 tbsp (60g) all-purpose flour
Filling
½ cup (100g) melted goiabada (sweet guava paste)

With a mixer, beat the eggs until doubling the volume. Add the sugar tablespoons, one by one. Add the flour in the same way. Spread the batter into a rectangular baking pan covered with a sheet of parchment paper greased with butter. Bake in a medium-low preheated oven for approximately 15 minutes, or until golden brown. After baking, sprinkle the cake with sugar and flip it over a clean and slightly damp cloth. Spread the melted goiabada and roll using the cloth to make the roll cake.

Servings: 10
Total time: 40 minutes
Difficulty: Easy

Acknowledgements

I thank the people of Trancoso who welcomed me so well, the friends I made here, the guests who turned into friends...

Also my life companions, my children and my work team.

Penha, Lú, Dani and Quéia

Credits

Creation of recipes:
Sandra Marques

Cover:
Cup designed by Ieda Sá

Capim Santo Kitchen:
Penha, Lu, Dani and Quéia

Photographs on page 2 and back cover:
Marcel Leite

CAPIMSANTO

Rua do Beco, 55 — Praça São João — Quadrado Histórico
45818-000 — Trancoso — BA — Brazil
+ 55 73 3668-1122 — capimsanto@capimsanto.com.br

Cook ♥ Lovers

Rua dos Italianos, 845 - Bom Retiro - 01131-000
São Paulo - SP - Brazil - + 55 11 3846-5141
contato@boccato.com.br
www.boccato.com.br - www.cooklovers.com.br

© Editora Boccato / CookLovers

Editing André Boccato

Editorial coordination Maria Aparecida C. Ramos

Testing of recipes Aline Maria Terrassi Leitão/Henrique Cortat

Proofreading Tatiana Raia (TopTexto)

Photographs André Boccato

Text collaboration Jezebel Salern

Commercial director Marcelo Nogueira

```
Dados Internacionais de Catalogação na Publicação (CIP)
       (Câmara Brasileira do Livro, SP, Brasil)

    Marques, Sandra
      Good morning Trancoso! : 40 breakfast recipes /
    Sandra Marques ; [tradução Tatiana Raia]. --
    São Paulo : Boccato, 2012.

      Título original: Bom dia Trancoso! 40 receitas
    para acompanhar o café da manhã.

      1. Culinária 2. Gastronomia 3. Receitas
    I. Título.


12-07626                                      CDD-641.5
```

Índices para catálogo sistemático:

1. Receitas : Culinária   641.5

Good Morning Trancoso!

40 breakfast recipes
by Sandra Marques

Cook ♥ Lovers

Good Morning Trancoso!

40 breakfast recipes
by Sandra Marques

summary

queijadinhas (traditional sweet with eggs and coconut)	9
lazy apple pie	10
"bom-bocado" with corn flour	13
white chocolate brownie with macadamia nuts	14
apple cake	17
rabanadas (sweet french toasts)	18
tapioca cake	21
passion fruit and coconut muffin	22
poppy seed cake	25
cinnamon rolls	26
lime cake	29
coffee cake	30
guava pastries	33
carrot cake	34
heart of palm "empada" (traditional small pie)	37
banana cake	38
cheese quiche	41
sweet tapioca fried dumplings	42

tapioca pudding	45
bom-bocado with sweet corn	46
pancakes	49
orange cake	50
chocolate brownie	53
Mixed cake	54
yogurt and lime pancakes	57
sonhos (brazilian doughnuts)	58
banana and white chocolate muffin	61
"anthill" cake (vanilla cake with chocolate sprinkles)	62
carrot cake with walnuts	65
chocolate cake	66
chocolate chip cookies	69
tapioca porridge	70
pão de queijo (cheese rolls)	73
madeleines	74
raisin cake	77
rice flour muffins with coconut	78
guava roll cake	81

presentation

My interest in cooking began early, by watching my mother making puddings that she would sell at my dad's ice cream parlor, my paternal grandmother and my aunts making goiabada (from the guavas they had gathered in a vacant lot next to our houses) or pots full of banana paste that would be used as filling for breads or cones.

If there was a party, the kids used to stand by the table to see my aunt preparing alfenim candies (alfenim is a sugary paste that is hardened) and it was pure magic! "What a treat it was to eat those tiny leftovers".

My maternal grandmother, who was Lebanese and a skilled cook, always made us a surprise with her Arab dishes or some new recipe from the collection she was gathering from the "Bom Apetite" (Good Appetite) magazine. This was a collection I soon inherited because I also loved collecting recipes!

But, it only became my livelihood when I arrived in Trancoso and started to sell whole grain bread and granola to survive...

Then, other types of cakes and sweets came along, which turned into treats. On those days, the young people who used to visit Trancoso came to my house to eat breakfast, and, naturally some years later the result was the restaurant and lodge Capim Santo.

queijadinhas (traditional sweet with eggs and coconut)

1 can (395g) sweetened condensed milk
3 eggs, 1 tbsp (20g) butter
2 cups (160g) desiccated shredded coconut

In a mixing bowl, mix eggs with sweetened condensed milk, butter and shredded coconut. Leave to rest for 10 minutes and distribute the batter in small cupcake paper cups, which should be already placed in muffin pans. Bake in a low preheated oven for approximately 35 minutes.

Servings: 7
Total time: 45 minutes
Difficulty: Easy

lazy apple pie

Filling: 8 apples, peeled and sliced
½ cup (80g) white sugar + 1 tbsp (20g) white sugar
2 tbsp (30ml) water, 3 eggs, whisked
1 cup (240ml) milk
ground cinnamon and butter to taste
Pastry: 3 cups (360g) all-purpose flour
1 ½ cup (240g) white sugar
1 cup (230g) butter
1 tbsp (12g) baking powder

Filling: Add the apples, ½ cup (80g) of sugar and water to a pan. Cook until the apple slices are soft. Remove from heat and set aside.

Mix the eggs with milk and 1 tablespoon (20g) of sugar. Set aside.

Grease a round pan with butter and set aside.

Pastry: In a mixing bowl, mix all of the pastry ingredients with your fingertips until it resembles coarse flour. Spread half of the pastry over the bottom of the pan and cover with half of the filling. Continue making layers alternating between laying the pastry and filling with the remaining ingredients. Pour the mixture of eggs and milk over the pie. Sprinkle with ground cinnamon and tiny pieces of butter. Leave to rest for 10 minutes. Bake in a medium preheated oven for approximately 1 hour.

Servings: 16
Total time: 1 hour and 20 minutes
Difficulty: Easy

"bom-bocado" with corn flour

4 cups (960ml) milk, 2 cups (320g) white sugar
4 eggs, 1 cup (120g) corn flour
1 tbsp (15g) all-purpose flour
½ cup (40g) grated Parmesan cheese
½ cup (40g) dehydrated shredded coconut
3 tbsp (45ml) melted butter
2 tbsp (24g) baking powder

Blend milk, sugar and eggs in a blender. Transfer the mixture to a mixing bowl and add cornmeal, flour, cheese, coconut, butter and baking powder. Mix. Pour the mixture into a greased baking pan or baking dish and sprinkled with corn flour. Bake in a medium preheated oven for approximately 45 minutes.

Servings: 15
Total time: 1 hour
Difficulty: Easy

white chocolate brownie with macadamia nuts

200g of white chocolate
½ cup (115g) unsalted butter, 2 eggs
1 cup (160g) white sugar, 1 tsp (5ml) vanilla extract
1 cup (120g) all-purpose flour, 1 tsp (5g) baking powder
a pinch of salt
½ cup (60g) chopped roasted macadamia nuts

Melt the white chocolate in a bowl over a pan of simmering water and add in the butter. Mix well, remove from heat and let it cool.

In a mixing bowl, beat the eggs with sugar and vanilla until it forms a light-colored cream. Add the chocolate and set aside.

In another mixing bowl, sift flour mixed with the baking powder and salt. Add the chocolate mixture and whisk until smooth. Add the macadamia nuts, stir and pour the batter into a greased and floured rectangular cake pan. Bake in a medium preheated oven for approximately 35 minutes, or stick a toothpick in the brownie; if it comes out moist, it is ready.

Cut into squares and serve.

Servings: 16
Total time: 1 hour
Difficulty: Easy

apple cake

4 cups peeled and grated apples
1 cup (140g) yellow raisins
1 cup (80g) ground walnuts
½ cup (120ml) cooking oil
1 ½ cups (240g) demerara sugar. 2 eggs
a pinch of salt. 1 tbsp (8g) ground cinnamon
1 tbsp (15ml) vanilla extract. 2 cups (240g) all-purpose
flour. 1 tsp (5g) baking soda. 1 tbsp (12g) baking powder

In a mixing bowl, mix the apples with raisins, walnuts, cooking oil, sugar, eggs, salt, cinnamon, vanilla, flour, baking soda and baking powder until it becomes a smooth batter. Pour the batter in a greased baking pan sprinkled with sugar and bake in a medium preheated oven for approximately 40 minutes.

Servings: 12
Total time: 1 hour
Difficulty: Easy

rabanadas
(sweet french toasts)

½ can (200g) sweetened condensed milk
100ml milk, 2 eggs, whisked
3 bread rolls, left to dry overnight
oil for frying
white sugar and ground cinnamon to taste

In a mixing bowl, mix together the sweetened condensed milk, whole milk and eggs. Set aside. Slice the bread in 0.5-inch-thick slices. Dip the slices in the egg and milk mixture and fry them in hot oil. Lay the slices over paper towel so that the oil is absorbed. Dip the slices in a mixture of sugar and cinnamon. Serve.

Servings: 15 slices
Total time: 15 minutes
Difficulty: Easy

tapioca cake

3 cups (450g) raw or cooked tapioca
1 ½ cup (360ml) coconut milk
1 cup (80g) desiccated shredded coconut
½ cup (115g) butter
1 ½ cup (240g) white sugar
3 eggs
1 tbsp (12g) baking powder

Grind the tapioca in a blender, little by little, so that it crumbles nicely. Transfer to a mixing bowl; add the coconut milk and the shredded coconut. Leave to rest for 20 minutes.

In another mixing bowl, whisk butter with sugar and add the eggs, one by one, until smooth. Add the tapioca mixture that was set aside and whisk a bit more. Pour in a greased and floured rectangular baking pan and bake in a medium preheated oven for approximately 40 minutes.

Servings: 12
Total time: 1 hour
Difficulty: Easy

passion fruit and coconut muffin

½ cup (115g) butter
1 cup (160g) white sugar, 3 eggs
1 ½ cup (180g) all-purpose flour
½ cup (120ml) milk, 1 tsp (5ml) vanilla extract
1 cup (80g) desiccated shredded coconut
Pulp of 2 passion fruits dehydrated, 1 tbsp (12g) baking powder

Using a mixer, mix butter, eggs (one at a time) and alternate flour with milk and vanilla. Add in coconut, passion fruit pulp and, finally, the baking powder.

Fill round paper cups with the batter until 2/3 full and insert them into the muffin pan.

Bake in a medium preheated oven for approximately 40 minutes.

Servings: 12
Total time: 1 hour
Difficulty: Easy

poppy seed cake

1 cup (160g) white sugar
4 eggs
1 cup (230g) butter
½ cup (120ml) milk
1 tbsp (15ml) vanilla extract
1 tsp (1g) grated lime zest
2 cups (240g) all-purpose flour
1 tbsp (12g) baking powder
½ tsp (4g) salt
½ cup (120ml) poppy seeds

With a mixer, beat sugar with egg yolks and butter. Add in milk, vanilla and lemon zest. Next, add flour, baking powder and salt.

Stop mixing and carefully add the poppy seeds and egg whites previously beaten until forming firm peaks. Pour in a greased and floured rectangular cake pan and bake in a medium preheated oven for approximately 40 minutes.

Servings: 12
Total time: 1 hour
Difficulty: Easy

cinnamon rolls

Pastry: 30g yeast
1 ½ cup (360ml) warm milk, ½ cup (80g) white sugar
4 cups (480g) all-purpose flour, 2 eggs, ½ cup (115g) butter
Filling: ½ cup (120ml) melted butter
1 cup (160g) white sugar
3 tbsp (24g) ground cinnamon

In a mixing bowl, dissolve the baking powder in milk with sugar. Cover with a cloth and leave to rest for approximately 15 minutes. In another bowl, add flour and make a hole in the center; add eggs, butter and the baking powder mixture that was set aside. Mix well and, if necessary, add a little more flour. Knead until the dough is elastic; cover with a cloth and leave it to rise for 1 hour to double its volume.

Remove the dough from the bowl and roll it out with a rolling pin in a flat surface sprinkled with flour, making a rectangle. Spread melted butter and a mixture of sugar and cinnamon and roll it up. Tighten the edges firmly and slice in 0.8-inch-thick (2cm) thick slices. Arrange the slices in a greased and floured baking pan, press lightly and bake in a medium preheated oven for approximately 30 minutes.

Servings: 15
Total time: 1 hour and 30 minutes
Difficulty: Medium

lime cake

1 ½ cup (240g) white sugar, 4 eggs
1 cup (230g) butter
2 cups (240g) all-purpose flour, 1 tbsp (3g) grated lime zest
1 cup (240ml) milk, 1 tbsp (12g) baking powder
Icing: 2 cups (260g) confectioner's sugar
4 tbsp (60ml) lime juice

With a mixer, beat sugar with egg yolks and butter. Add flour, lime zests, milk and, finally, baking powder and the egg whites previously beaten until you have firm peaks. Pour in a greased and floured rectangular (12x16.5in/31x42cm) baking pan and bake in a medium preheated oven for approximately 40 minutes.

Icing: Mix the confectioner's sugar with lime juice. Pour over the cake while still warm, in the baking pan. Cut the cake into squares and let it cool to dry the frosting.

Servings: 12
Total time: 1 hour
Difficulty: Easy

coffee cake

2 cups (480ml) coffee
2 cups (320g) white sugar
2 tbsp (36g) cocoa powder
½ cup (115g) butter
2 eggs
1 tsp (5ml) vanilla extract
2 cups (240g) all-purpose flour
2 tsp (5g) baking powder
½ tsp (2g) salt
½ tsp (1g) ground cloves

In a pan, add coffee, sugar and powdered chocolate. Simmer in low heat for 10 minutes. Remove from heat and let cool.

With a mixer, mix butter, eggs (one at a time), vanilla and then add the cold coffee mixture. Add flour, baking powder, salt and cloves. Pour in a greased and floured rectangular cake pan and bake in a medium preheated oven for approximately 40 minutes.

Servings: 12
Total time: 1 hour
Difficulty: Easy

guava pastries

2 cups (240g) all-purpose flour
½ cup (80g) white sugar
1 egg, ½ cup (115g) butter
1 tbsp (15ml) water
1 ½ cup (300g) goiabada (sweet guava paste), diced
confectioner's sugar for sprinkling

In a mixing bowl, mix flour, sugar, egg, butter and water until smooth. Using a rolling pin, roll out the pastry until it is 0.2 inches (0.5cm) thick and then cut it in circles with a round pastry cutter. Place some goiabada cubes in the center of each circle and close it tightly, pressing the edges with a fork. Bake in a medium preheated oven for approximately 30 minutes. Remove from the oven and sprinkle with confectioner's sugar.

Servings: 20
Total time: 50 minutes
Difficulty: Easy

carrot cake

5 eggs, 2 cups (320g) white sugar
1 cup (240ml) cooking oil, 3 chopped carrots
3 cups (360g) all-purpose flour, ½ tbsp (6g) baking soda
1 tbsp (12g) baking powder
Frosting: 1 cup (240ml) milk, 1 cup (160g) white sugar
1 cup (110g) cocoa powder, 1 tbsp (20g) butter

Blend eggs, sugar, oil and carrots in a blender. In a mixing bowl, mix flour, baking soda and baking powder. Add the blended mixture and mix well. Pour in a greased and floured rectangular cake pan and bake in a medium preheated oven for approximately 40 minutes.

Frosting: In a pan, mix milk, sugar, and chocolate and cook until thick. Before removing from heat, add butter. Stir well and spread over the baked cake. Cut into squares and serve.

Servings: 16
Total time: 1 hour
Difficulty: Easy

heart of palm "empada" (traditional small pie)

Pastry: 3 cups (360g) all-purpose flour
2 egg yolks, 1 ¼ cup (290g) butter, salt to taste
1 tsp (5g) baking powder
Filling: 1 tbsp (15ml) olive oil
½ onion, minced, 1 garlic clove, minced
2 cups (140g) chopped heart of palm
1 tomato, peeled, seedless and chopped
salt, pepper and parsley to taste, 1 cup (240ml) milk
1 tbsp (8g) cornstarch, 1 egg yolk for egg wash

Pastry: In a mixing bowl, add flour, egg yolks, butter, salt and baking powder. Knead until obtaining a smooth dough. Set aside.

Filling: In a pan, heat olive oil and fry onion and garlic. Add chopped heart of palm, tomato and seasonings (salt, pepper, parsley) to taste. Finally, dissolve cornstarch in milk and pour into the pan. Stir until it thickens. Remove from heat and set aside.

Spread the pastry in empada baking tins (or small muffin tins), add the filling (which should be cold) and close with a disc of pastry. Brush with egg wash and bake in a medium preheated oven for approximately 30 minutes, or until golden brown.

Servings: 12 medium pies
Total time: 1 hour
Difficulty: Easy

banana cake

1 cup (160g) white sugar
½ cup (115g) butter
4 eggs, ½ cup (120ml) milk
2 cups (240g) all-purpose flour
1 tbsp (12g) baking powder
½ tsp (2g) salt, 6 bananas, sliced
sugar and ground cinnamon for sprinkling

With a mixer, beat sugar with butter and egg yolks until forming a light-colored cream. Add milk, alternating with flour, baking powder and salt. Beat the egg whites until firm and fold into the batter. Pour half the batter into a greased and floured baking pan and cover with half of the sliced bananas. Pour in the remaining batter and finish with the bananas. Sprinkle with sugar, cinnamon and bake in a medium preheated oven for approximately 40 minutes or until golden brown. Let it cool and cut into squares.

Servings: 16
Total time: 1 hour
Difficulty: Easy

cheese quiche

Pastry: 1 ½ cup (180g) all-purpose flour
½ cup (115g) cold butter
1 egg
2 tbsp (30ml) iced water
salt to taste
Filling: 3 eggs, whisked
1 ½ cup (360ml) milk
1 cup (80g) grated Parmesan cheese
salt and pepper to taste

Pastry: In a mixing bowl, knead flour with cold butter, egg and water until the dough is smooth and doesn't stick in your hands. Roll out the dough and transfer it to a baking pan (11in/28cm diameter) with a removable bottom, trim the edges, make holes in the bottom with a fork and bake in a medium preheated oven for 10 minutes. Remove from the oven and set aside.

Filling: In a mixing bowl, whisk eggs with milk, Parmesan cheese, salt and pepper to taste. Pour inside the quiche and bake again at medium heat for approximately 25 minutes.

Servings: 8
Total time: 1 hour
Difficulty: Easy

sweet tapioca fried dumplings

1 cup (240ml) water
1 cup (240ml) coconut milk
½ cup (80g) white sugar
1 ½ cup (225g) tapioca
½ tsp (2g) salt
½ cup (40g) dehydrated shredded coconut
oil for frying
sugar and ground cinnamon for sprinkling

In a pan, add water, coconut milk and sugar. Cook until it starts to boil.

In a mixing bowl, add tapioca, salt and coconut. Pour in the boiled liquid and let it rest for 30 minutes until the tapioca is swelled and soft. With wet hands, take pieces of the dough and make somewhat long dumplings. Deep-fry them in oil until golden brown. Remove and place them over sheets of paper towel to drain off the oil. Sprinkle the dumplings with sugar and cinnamon. Serve.

Servings: 9
Total time: 45 minutes
Difficulty: Easy

tapioca pudding

3 cups (720ml) water
2 cups (480ml) coconut milk
3 cups (450g) tapioca
1 cup (160g) white sugar
Topping
1 can (395g) sweetened condensed milk
1 cup (80g) dehydrated shredded coconut

In a pan, add water and coconut milk and bring to a boil.

In a mixing bowl, add tapioca and sugar. Pour the boiled mixture and let rest for approximately 30 minutes. Transfer to a baking pan and, when you remove it from the pan, cover with sweetened condensed milk and sprinkle with shredded coconut.

Servings: 10
Total time: 50 minutes
Difficulty: Easy

bom-bocado with sweet corn

1 can (200g) canned sweet corn
1 can (395g) sweetened condensed milk
3 eggs
2 tbsp (30ml) melted butter
3 tbsp (30g) all-purpose flour
sugar and ground cinnamon for sprinkling

Blend the corn kernels in a blender and sieve. Set aside.

Return the sieved corn juice to the blender and blend with sweet condensed milk, eggs, flour and blend until smooth.

Pour into paper cups (which should be inside the cups of a small muffin pan), sprinkle them with cinnamon and bake in bain-marie, in a medium preheated oven for approximately 40 minutes.

Servings: 10
Total time: 1 hour
Difficulty: Easy

pancakes

1 cup (240ml) milk
1 cup (120g) all-purpose flour
1 egg
salt to taste

Blend milk, flour, eggs and salt in a blender until smooth.

Cook small doses of the batter in a non-stick frying pan or pancake pan.

Servings: 10
Total time: 30 minutes
Difficulty: Easy

orange cake

4 eggs
1 cup (240ml) cooking oil
2 cups (320g) white sugar
1 orange, whole but seedless, sliced in 4 wedges
2 cups (240g) all-purpose flour
1 tbsp (12g) baking powder
Syrup
1 cup (240ml) orange juice
1 cup (160g) white sugar

Blend eggs with oil, sugar and orange in a blender. Set aside.

In a mixing bowl, add flour and baking powder and add the previously blended mixture. Mix thoroughly and pour in a greased and floured round tube cake pan and bake in a medium preheated oven for approximately 40 minutes.

Syrup: In a pan, mix orange juice with sugar and bring to a boil for 5 minutes. Pour the syrup over the cake and serve.

Servings: 12
Total time: 1 hour
Difficulty: Easy

chocolate brownie

1 cup (230g) butter
2 cups (320g) white sugar
4 eggs
120g medium dark chocolate, melted
1 tsp (5ml) vanilla extract
1 cup (120g) all-purpose flour
1 cup (145g) chopped Brazil nuts

With a mixer, mix the butter and sugar. Add eggs one by one, the melted chocolate, vanilla, flour and nuts.
Mix thoroughly and pour in a greased and floured small rectangular cake pan and bake in a medium preheated oven for approximately 45 minutes.

Servings: 10
Total time: 1 hour
Difficulty: Easy

mixed cake

½ cup (115g) butter
1 cup (160g) white sugar
2 eggs
2 cups (240g) all-purpose flour
1 cup (240ml) milk
1 tsp (5ml) vanilla extract
1 tbsp (12g) baking powder
1 tbsp (8g) ground cinnamon
½ tsp (1g) ground cloves
3 tbsp (78g) sugarcane molasses

With a mixer, blend the butter and sugar until obtaining a light-colored cream. Add the eggs, one by one and then add flour, milk, vanilla and baking powder. Mix thoroughly.

Set a small portion of the batter aside and add cinnamon, cloves and molasses to it. Pour the remaining batter into a greased floured rectangular baking pan (20x30cm/9x13in) and lightly mix with the spice batter. Bake in a medium preheated oven for approximately 40 minutes.

Servings: 12
Total time: 1 hour
Difficulty: Easy

yogurt and lime pancakes

1 egg
1 cup (240ml) yogurt
2 tbsp (30ml) melted butter
2 tbsp (30ml) white sugar
1 cup (120g) all-purpose flour
1 tbsp (12g) baking powder
grated lime zest of 1 whole lime

With a mixer, beat the egg with yogurt, butter and sugar. Add flour, baking powder and lime zest. Mix thoroughly. Grease a non-stick frying pan with a bit of oil, heat it and add a serving of the batter. When it starts to make bubbles, flip the pancake and cook the other side until golden brown. Repeat this process until using up all batter.

Servings: 6
Total time: 1 hour
Difficulty: Easy

sonhos (brazilian doughnuts)

30g yeast, ½ cup (80g) white sugar, 1 cup (240ml) warm milk
4 cups (480g) all-purpose flour, 1 tsp (4g) salt
3 tbsp (45ml) butter, oil for frying
Filling: 2 cups (480ml) milk, 1 tsp (5ml) vanilla extract
½ cup (80g) white sugar, 4 egg yolks, 3 tbsp (24g) cornstarch
white sugar for sprinkling

In a mixing bowl, dissolve yeast in milk with sugar. In another mixing bowl, add flour and salt. Open a cavity in the center and add in the dissolved yeast and butter. Knead until smooth and elastic. Cover the bowl with a cloth and let it rest until doubling the volume.

Using a rolling pin, roll out the pastry until it is 0.5 inches (1cm) thick and then cut it in medium-sized circles with a round pastry cutter. Transfer the pastry circles to a baking pan sprinkled with flour and allow growing again for approximately 30 minutes. Heat the oil in a pan and deep-fry the cakes over low heat, until it is golden brown and double the volume. Lay over sheets of paper towel to drain off the oil.

Filling: In a pan, mix milk, vanilla, sugar, egg yolks and cornstarch. Cook over low heat, stirring until thick. Slice the cakes in half, without totally cutting the two halves apart, fill with the cream (after cooling down), and sprinkle with sugar.

Servings: 16
Total time: 1 hour and 15 minutes
Difficulty: Medium

banana and white chocolate muffin

½ cup (115g) butter
1 cup (160g) white sugar
3 eggs
½ cup (120ml) milk
3 cups (360g) all-purpose flour
3 bananas, mashed
1 tbsp (12g) baking powder
1 cup (160g) chopped white chocolate

With a mixer, mix the butter with sugar and the eggs, one by one. Add flour, alternating with milk. Add mashed bananas and baking powder. Fill round paper cups with the batter until 2/3 full and insert them into the muffin pan and, finally, sprinkle with chopped white chocolate. Bake in a medium preheated oven for approximately 40 minutes.

Servings: 9
Total time: 50 minutes
Difficulty: Easy

"anthill" cake (vanilla cake with chocolate sprinkles)

½ cup (115g) butter
1 cup (160g) white sugar
3 eggs
2 cups (240g) all-purpose flour
1 cup (240ml) milk
1 tbsp (15ml) vanilla extract
1 tbsp (12g) baking powder
1 cup (100g) chocolate sprinkles

With a mixer, mix the butter and sugar until obtaining a light-colored cream. Add the egg yolks while still mixing. Add flour, milk, vanilla, baking powder and mix a bit more. Add chocolate sprinkles to the batter and fold the egg whites beaten into stiff peaks. Pour in a greased and floured round tube cake pan and bake in a medium preheated oven for approximately 40 minutes.

Servings: 12
Total time: 1 hour
Difficulty: Easy

carrot cake with walnuts

1 ½ cup (240g) white sugar
1 cup (240ml) cooking oil, 3 eggs
1 ½ cup (180g) all-purpose flour
1 tsp (2g) ground cinnamon
1 tbsp (15ml) vanilla extract
2 ½ tsp (9g) baking powder
½ cup (40g) ground walnuts
2 cups (170g) grated carrots
Frosting: 2 cups (480g) cream cheese
2 cups (460g) unsalted butter
2 cups (260g) confectioner's sugar
1 tsp (5ml) vanilla extract

With a mixer, mix sugar with oil. Add the eggs one by one, flour, cinnamon, vanilla, baking powder, walnuts and, finally, the carrots. Pour in a greased and floured round cake pan and bake in a medium preheated oven for approximately 40 minutes. Remove from the oven, let cool and remove from the pan.

Frosting: With a mixer, whip cream cheese, butter, sugar and vanilla until firm. Decorate the cake.

Servings: 12
Total time: 1 hour
Difficulty: Easy

chocolate cake

1 cup (160g) white sugar
1 cup (130g) unsalted butter
5 eggs
2 ½ cup (300g) all-purpose flour
1 cup (240ml) milk
1 ½ cup (165g) cocoa powder
1 tbsp (12g) baking powder
Syrup
1 cup (240ml) milk
¼ cup (60ml) rum
2 tbsp (30ml) white sugar
3 tbsp (54g) cocoa powder

With a mixer, mix the butter with sugar and egg yolks until obtaining a light-colored cream. Add flour and milk. Continue to mix as you add cocoa powder, baking powder and, finally, fold egg whites in firm peaks. Pour in a greased and floured rectangular baking pan and bake in a medium preheated oven for approximately 40 minutes.

Syrup: In a pan, mix milk, rum, sugar and powdered chocolate. Cook over low heat and let it boil, stirring occasionally until thick. Pour over the cake while hot.

Servings: 12
Total time: 1 hour
Difficulty: Easy

chocolate chip cookies

1 cup (170g) demerara sugar
1 cup (130g) unsalted butter
1 tsp (5ml) vanilla extract
1 egg
1 ½ cup (180g) all-purpose flour
1 tsp (5g) baking powder
1 ¼ cup (200g) chocolate chips

With a mixer, mix the butter with sugar and vanilla until obtaining a light-colored cream. Add the egg, mix well and add flour and baking powder. Finally, add chocolate chips. In a baking pan covered with a sheet of parchment paper, distribute spoonfuls of the dough, leaving some space between the cookies because they will expand. Bake in a medium preheated oven for approximately 10 minutes, or until the edges of the cookies are golden brown. Remove the pan from the oven and let the cookies cool down before taking them off the pan.

Servings: 50 small cookies
Total time: 1 hour
Difficulty: Easy

tapioca porridge

1 ½ cup (225g) tapioca
2 cups (480ml) coconut milk
2 cups (160g) dehydrated shredded coconut
1 ½ cup (240g) white sugar
2 cups (480ml) water or milk
ground cinnamon for sprinkling

In a mixing bowl, soak the tapioca in coconut milk for 10 minutes. Afterwards, cook with coconut, sugar and milk or water, adding the liquid slowly and stirring until obtaining a dense cream. When it's ready, sprinkle the porridge with ground cinnamon.

Servings: 8
Total time: 30 minutes
Difficulty: Easy

pão de queijo (cheese rolls)

3 cups (450g) sweet manioc starch
½ cup (150g) sour manioc starch
½ tbsp (12g) salt
½ cup (120ml) cooking oil
1 ½ cup (360ml) milk
3 eggs
4 cups (320g) grated hard cheese

In a mixing bowl, mix sweet and sour manioc starch and salt.

In a pan, heat up milk with oil. When it starts to boil, pour the liquid over the manioc starch mix and slowly mix with a spoon. Add eggs and knead for approximately 10 minutes, until smooth. Add cheese and mix thoroughly with your hand, make little balls of dough and distribute them over a baking pan previously greased with oil. Leave some distance between them so they won't stick together when they expand. Bake in a medium preheated oven for approximately 25 minutes, or until the cheese rolls start to become golden brown.

Servings: 80 small rolls
Total time: 1 hour
Difficulty: Easy

madeleines

1 cup (160g) white sugar
1 tbsp (26g) honey
6 egg yolks
1 egg
1 cup (230g) butter
1 cup (135g) potato starch
1 cup (120g) all-purpose flour
6 egg whites
½ tbsp (2g) grated orange zest

With a mixer, beat sugar with egg yolks, honey and egg. Add butter and mix. Add potato starch and flour. When the batter is smooth fold in the egg whites in firm peaks and orange zest.

Pour the batter into an appropriate madeleine pan and bake in a medium-low preheated oven for approximately 20 minutes, or until golden brown.

Servings: 10
Total time: 1 hour
Difficulty: Easy

raisin cake

1 ½ cup (190g) brown sugar
1 cup (230g) butter
5 eggs
½ cup (120ml) sugarcane molasses
½ cup (120ml) milk
2 ½ cup (300g) all-purpose flour
1 tbsp (12g) baking powder
1 tsp (2g) ground cinnamon
½ tsp (1g) ground nutmeg
1 cup (140g) black raisins
1 cup (140g) yellow raisins
1 cup (130g) mixed candied fruits

With a mixer, mix the butter and sugar. Add egg yolks one by one and mix well. Add in molasses, milk, flour, baking powder, cinnamon, nutmeg and mix a bit more. Finally, fold the egg whites beaten into firm peaks. Carefully add raisins and candied fruits (flour the fruits before mixing into the batter). Pour in a greased and floured cake pan and bake in a medium-low preheated oven for approximately 1 hour.

Servings: 12
Total time: 1 hour
Difficulty: Easy

rice flour muffins with coconut

1 cup (160g) white sugar
1 cup (230g) butter
5 eggs
1 cup (80g) dehydrated shredded coconut
½ tsp (2g) salt
1 cup (150g) rice flour
1 tsp (5g) baking powder
shredded coconut for sprinkling

With a mixer, mix the butter and sugar. Add egg yolks one by one and mix well. Add shredded coconut, salt, rice flour and baking powder. Mix until smooth. Finally, fold the egg whites beaten into firm peaks. Fill 2/3 of greased and floured muffin cups with the batter and sprinkle with shredded coconut. Bake in a medium preheated oven for approximately 40 minutes.

Servings: 8
Total time: 1 hour
Difficulty: Easy

guava roll cake

6 eggs
6 tbsp (72g) white sugar
6 tbsp (60g) all-purpose flour
Filling
½ cup (100g) melted goiabada (sweet guava paste)

With a mixer, beat the eggs until doubling the volume. Add the sugar tablespoons, one by one. Add the flour in the same way. Spread the batter into a rectangular baking pan covered with a sheet of parchment paper greased with butter. Bake in a medium-low preheated oven for approximately 15 minutes, or until golden brown. After baking, sprinkle the cake with sugar and flip it over a clean and slightly damp cloth. Spread the melted goiabada and roll using the cloth to make the roll cake.

Servings: 10
Total time: 40 minutes
Difficulty: Easy

Acknowledgements

I thank the people of Trancoso who welcomed me so well, the friends I made here, the guests who turned into friends...

Also my life companions, my children and my work team.

Penha, Lú, Dani and Quéia

Credits

Creation of recipes:
Sandra Marques

Cover:
Cup designed by Ieda Sá

Capim Santo Kitchen:
Penha, Lu, Dani and Quéia

Photographs on page 2 and back cover:
Marcel Leite

CAPIMSANTO

Rua do Beco, 55 — Praça São João — Quadrado Histórico
45818-000 — Trancoso — BA — Brazil
+ 55 73 3668-1122 — capimsanto@capimsanto.com.br

Cook ♥ Lovers

Rua dos Italianos, 845 – Bom Retiro – 01131-000
São Paulo – SP – Brazil – +55 11 3846-5141
contato@boccato.com.br
www.boccato.com.br · www.cooklovers.com.br

© Editora Boccato / CookLovers

Editing André Boccato

Editorial coordination Maria Aparecida C. Ramos

Testing of recipes Aline Maria Terrassi Leitão/Henrique Cortat

Proofreading Tatiana Raia (TopTexto)

Photographs André Boccato

Text collaboration Jezebel Salern

Commercial director Marcelo Nogueira

Dados Internacionais de Catalogação na Publicação (CIP)
(Câmara Brasileira do Livro, SP, Brasil)

Marques, Sandra
  Good morning Trancoso! : 40 breakfast recipes /
Sandra Marques ; [tradução Tatiana Raia]. --
São Paulo : Boccato, 2012.

  Título original: Bom dia Trancoso! 40 receitas
para acompanhar o café da manhã.

  1. Culinária 2. Gastronomia 3. Receitas
I. Título.

12-07626   CDD-641.5

Índices para catálogo sistemático:

1. Receitas : Culinária   641.5